# LEARNING TO LIVE ONE GOLF SWING AT A TIME

J. Lang

BALBOA.
PRESS

A DIVISION OF HAY HOUSE

ISBN: 978-1-4525-5407-5 (sc)
ISBN: 978-1-4525-5408-2 (e)

Library of Congress Control Number: 2012910958

Balboa Press books may be ordered through booksellers or by contacting:

Balboa Press
A Division of Hay House
1663 Liberty Drive
Bloomington, IN 47403
www.balboapress.com
1-(877) 407-4847

Printed in the United States of America

Balboa Press rev. date: 07/23/12

# DEDICATION

To my wife and daughter: I thank you for your love and support. Each day you are my "starters."

For my dad, whose unfailing love for me and ever-changing love for the game of golf inspired me to write this collection.

To my very best friend, Rod: through birdies and bogies you have been like a brother to me. If we could only do something about your putting. Just kidding, Rod!

To the men and women of Tanglewood Golf Course, in Milton; Stonebrook Golf Club, in Pace; Travis Air Force Base's Cypress Lakes; Eglin Air Force Base's Eagle and Falcon; Rheinblick and Bitburgerland, in Germany; Kadena Air Base's Banyan Tree Golf Course; and to everyone I have played this amazing game with in between: each of you has shaped my life and taught me *How to Live One Golf Swing at a Time.*

# CONTENTS

# Preface

WELCOME TO MY COURSE. I am very excited to unveil a new design for you in the pages ahead. This course will challenge every player who dares "tee it up." The holes on this course are ever changing. As the course architect, I am always willing to tweak my work, and I've been threatening a grand redesign for years. It's not so much that I regret all this handiwork but just that, like most people, I have a memory that artistically "touches up" the past, and the future is always a blank page.

This course is played out in the daily walk of life. I could probably build a few courses for us to play with all of the life-imitates-golf lessons available to us, but I will only lay one course before you now. You are welcome to substitute your own scorecard and even think about the shot you might have hit instead of the one I played in a certain situation. You see, that's the beauty of the game: It's not really *how*. It's how *many*.

Golf is relative. We are all at different stages in development. That being said, I really do believe we can learn from anyone. It is my hope that laying my golf course before you will challenge you to create your own and cause you to reflect on the things you have really learned through the game of golf—the important things one must learn in this game of life.

Finally, as you play, remember to enjoy the walk. Don't rush, but don't stand still and let others pass you by.

Joey

# ACKNOWLEDGMENTS

I would like to thank the following people for making my journey through the game of golf more memorable and educational.

Aunt Iris, you introduced me to golf. My wife is still unhappy about that.

Debbie Joyce, you took a chance on an aspiring golf professional. Thanks!

Derek, Bruce, and Marjan, get the Mickey Mouse ball ready—it's all yours, Marjan! The Monday matches with you guys were the finest I have ever been a part of.

The staff and players at Woodlawn Golf Course at Ramstein Air Base, Germany: From the pro shop to the flight-line, "Happy to be here, proud to serve" is a way of life.

To the men and women of Tanglewood Golf Club: I could never be lucky enough to find such an amazing group at any other course.

To the staff and players of Banyan Tree Golf Course in Okinawa, Japan: thank you for trusting me with your golf swings. To the gaggle, "Roll it!" To Jeff, Sean, and Keith, "Next summer, let's get the band back together."

To the staff and players at Eglin Air Force Base Golf Courses: I will never forget my time there—but please get the ski lift fixed before I get back.

Doug, you are a great friend—keep moving forward.

The participants of our annual family golf trip: Can I just get one win? I vote we play scratch next year.

Jared Floyd, I can't describe your power better than Doug, so I won't.

Jesse, Johnny, Banks, Beach, Joe, Curtis, Jeff, Smitty, Nelly and Dave C, save me a spot in the captain's game

To John Deere Golf Division, I am still playing this game because of your commitment to safety.

To the players of The Princess Mary's Hospital Golf Club: in the middle of a war, I found peace playing your course. May every golfer know a place like TPMHGC.

Brad, Leann, Zach, and Nicholas, you guys are the most awesome golfing family in the world.

# HOLE #1, PAR 5:

## THE STARTER

I ALWAYS APPRECIATE A good par five to get things going. There seems to be a calmer version of me standing on the first tee when I am looking down the fairway of a reachable par five shortly after the starter calls my name. Golfers, you know who I am talking about. The starter is that old retired guy in the little booth (with bad fluorescent lighting) who believes himself to wield unbelievable power over walk-on golfers. Yeah, he's that poor sucker with the thankless job of pairing the swearing crowd with the club throwers. What a great job. If only it paid enough to keep the lights on.

"The starter" is an obvious title, since without a visit to the starter's shack you don't get to play the game. In life it's not too different. In my life, there are really so many people who could carry this title. As far as golf is concerned, that title would have to be bestowed on my aunt Iris. She is the one who carried a bright-eyed, super-excited brat to his very first day on the links. I remember so much about that day that I could fill volumes—and so little about everything else at the time that it's scary. My parents were divorcing, and golf was an escape from the reality of that, if only for a little while at a time.

We were headed to play a little course in Dillon, South Carolina. My aunt was a member there, and she knew she could talk the pro shop clerk into allowing me on the course during ladies' day. I was going to caddie, according to her, and she would not let the course marshal say one bad thing about it, or he would risk losing her membership to another course. If I never said thank you to her about that, let me do that now.

Thank you, Aunt Iris.

So, at seven years of age, I was to caddie for a woman who knew her home course better than I knew my times tables—which may still be the case. I loaded her six-thousand-pound golf bag onto the cart, and off we went.

I don't remember the first hole. I wasn't playing, but I do remember checking in with the starter. To a seven-year-old, he was a god. You couldn't play on the finest grass on the planet without his initials on your receipt. He was the gateway to the course, and Aunt Iris was my gateway to golf.

When we got to the second hole, she looked over at me and said, "Are you gonna hit?"

Faster than I ever opened any Christmas present, I was on that tee box. I put my never-before-used Titleist ball on top of my never-before-used tee. I took a mighty lash at the ball and heard my aunt exclaim, "Damn!"

I don't think she knew I heard her, but that's right—the first word I heard after the first time I hit a ball on the golf course was a cuss word. She said it because I outdrove her in front of her friends. I heard it because no one in my family is any good at whispering.

And so we played. My first round of golf was sixteen holes. I didn't play the first or last holes, because those holes were too near the clubhouse and I wasn't a paying player. Maybe one of these days I'll go back and drop a twenty in the junior-program donation box.

The highlight of that day was a holed bunker shot on the tenth hole. I heard another choice word from my aunt, but this time it was either because I beat her on the hole or because I ran around that bunker celebrating so much that the rake job was going to take five minutes. She never yelled at me for that, but after she made me rake the bunker, I realized tracking up the sand trap was not the right way to celebrate.

You see, golf is full of lessons just like that bunker lesson from my aunt. It was that simple act of raking an entire bunker that helped me to respect the work done by others. I had never met the man who raked that trap before I played that day. Chances are he is no longer alive (it's been twenty-five years since then), but I learned that, throughout our lives, people work behind the scenes for our enjoyment, our safety, and our freedom. From the starter who sends us on our way to the maintenance crew who makes the course playable (I didn't say fair), may we always remember to respect the men and women who make our lives more complete.

I am eternally indebted to my aunt for helping me find the game of golf. It is through her that I found something I can be passionate in pursuing, yet if I want to, I can also just go out on a Sunday afternoon with my dad and lose a few balls.

People say golf is just a game. I only hope that golf takes hold of them as it did me. This "game" will get inside you. It will make you laugh, cry, cuss, pray, make deals with God for a putt to fall, blame a mosquito for farting in your backswing, and so many other things you'd never trade for anything. Some of my best and worst moments ever have come on a golf course. I am really looking forward to the other seventeen holes we have to play together.

## HOLE #1 SWING KEYS:

Who is your starter? Who will get you in the game? If you're waiting for clearance to play, stop waiting. Whatever you are doing with your life—or your game, for that matter—will never be completed if it is not started. I am not here to dish out advice. You have to pay your own green fee in life. I am not pretending that writing a book makes it okay for me to tell you to jump right in and grab your dreams. What I *am* telling you is that you need to make a decision and enjoy the round, and if you get paired up with the swearing club thrower, duck!

# Hole #2, Par 4:

## SCORECARD AND A PENCIL

As I was playing my local club last week, something hit me that, as I look back, should have registered well before I thought about writing down all these bits about how life imitates golf into book form. I was dumbfounded at just how many places my local club offers a golfer a chance to pick up a scorecard and a pencil.

As I purchased some tees and a new glove for the round, I noticed that a holder full of both scorecards and pencils was sitting next to the register . Did I grab one of each? No, I merely collected my change and went to check in with the starter.

"Hi, Joe," I said as I handed my yellow starter copy to the weekend first-tee attendant.

"Good morning, Joe," he said back to me with the enthusiasm reserved for a funeral. It was a beautiful morning, and I knew he would have rather spent it playing golf than counting the number of weekend warriors with pipe dreams of driving the first green.

As Joe handed me back my initialed copy of the receipt, I looked down at the box of scorecards on the ledge of the starter shack. Did I grab one? No, not this time either. I took for granted that the cart crew would place one on the steering wheel under the clip designed for scorecards and pencils.

After loading up the cart and teeing off, I noticed that there was no scorecard on the cart. Being a nice guy, I didn't want to delay the group behind me more than required, so I refused to take the ten steps back to the starter shack for a scorecard.

"Just get one at the second-tee mailbox, kid," I muttered to myself.

I proceeded to knock my second shot stiff and made the birdie.

"Now I have to keep score," I said to my putter. Since I had made the putt, I was on speaking terms with my flat stick. I did let my putter know at that time that it was instantly replaceable should it decide to go cold on me.

So our group pulled up to the second tee. Sitting next to the tee was a ball washer, a water cooler, and the mailbox of scorecards and pencils. Did I grab one? Heck, no. I had to make sure no one stole my honors. Don't jump in front of my birdie, or you might wake up with a divot on your pillow. I hit my tee shot just a little left of right center and ran back to the cart. Hole number two was a reachable par five, and I needed to hit that second ball before I lost my swing. So let's get moving, boys.

Halfway down the fairway, I realized I still hadn't gotten a scorecard. What a ——! (Insert choice golf expletive here.)

It was just after I missed the green with my second shot that I realized that not having the scorecard was actually becoming a distraction. I don't know why. I think, more than anything, that I realized how many chances I'd had to get one and still hadn't done it.

Finally, the drink-cart girl came by on the fourth hole. To my surprise, the course keeps about twenty cards and pencils stocked on the drink cart for guys having mornings like the one I was having. I paid for our drinks and made sure to grab two scorecards and two pencils, one for today and one for the bag—just in case I ever have another bypass morning.

# HOLE #2 SWING KEYS:

There are two main thoughts I have for this reading.

Are you more like the course? Do you give people so many chances to get what they need from you that you actually create more work for yourself? It takes someone more than just a few minutes each day to reload scorecards in all the places my local course puts them for golfers to grab. I'm not saying that it's wrong to be nice to people, but really, how many chances did I miss to get the thing I needed at that moment? Personal responsibility has to come into play sometime, or so you would think.

Are you going through life as I went through the early part of my round the other day? Do you neglect to realize how many people in your life are there trying to help you? Do you forget to see all the places in your life where what you need is set out right there in front of you?

On this day, golf taught me to respect a little more the time others invest in me. Nothing in life is an accident. People reach out to us all the time. Do we overlook them? Do we even realize they are there for us?

# HOLE #3 PAR 4:

## UNLUCKY PRECISION

THE OTHER DAY, I was playing with a student of mine at Banyan Tree Golf Course, in Okinawa, Japan. Phil O. was in for his nine-hole playing lesson, and he wanted to discuss strategy for an upcoming tournament.

As I watched Phil hit his second shot, I thought to myself that now would be a good time to discuss the concept of safe shots versus flagsticks that you should fire at. He was playing overly cautiously, and I think it was what Phil thought I wanted him to do.

"Phil, I believe that was a good pin to shoot at. You had a good angle and no danger left or right. Also, the slope of the green would have still rewarded a shot that went a little long." I told him this as I grabbed a club and prepared to hit my own shot.

"Well, Joey, I didn't want you to get on me for flag hunting this early in the round." His reply came with a little barb on it.

"I know I said you couldn't win a three-day tournament on the first day, but you could lose it, Phil, so you still have to pick spots to produce. There are going to be places every day of the tournament that will tempt you to a little more aggressive line, and there will be pin locations that you will not be able to fire at. I want you to examine the opportunities as they come and ask yourself, "Will the aggressive shot invite trouble?" If the answer is no, Phil, I want you to fire at the hole. If a mistake on an aggressive shot brings a big number into play, hit it to the fat part of the green and smile when you walk away with par."

"Okay, Joey, but you know I'm going to beat you the rest of the round."

"I hope you do, Phil. But you'd better be prepared to earn it, because this pin is calling my name."

I lined up my shot, determined to show my student the line I wished he had taken moments earlier. I hit the shot crisply and watched the ball take off toward the pin. The ball descended right on the mark. Neither Phil nor I spoke as we watched the ball head straight for the cup.

Whack! The ball hit the flagstick and ricocheted twenty feet down hill and slightly right of the green. In a moment, I had gone from elation at the thought of holing a shot from the fairway for eagle to the slightly gut-punched feeling of getting up and down from heavy rough.

Phil and I looked at each other and laughed. "Where did that fit into your assessment of the opportunity?" he asked.

Crickets chirped. I had no witty response to his question, so I let it die. I got up-and-down for par to validate my "aggressive line didn't create trouble" theory and shook my head as we walked over to the fourth-tee box.

After a couple of days, I finally had the response for Phil that I felt the shot had warranted. Many times in life, and golf, we set goals or targets. Nobody, I hope, sets these objectives without the true intent of reaching them. The pin was not my target, the hole was. Hitting the pin indicated that my direction was true but that I had overshot my goal. A foot shorter and I would have been celebrating eagle. A foot longer and I would have flown over the stick without hitting it and the ball come to rest in easy birdie range, maybe even spinning back into the hole for eagle. The fact is, we were both impressed with the shot at the time—it was just "unlucky precision," as Phil called it.

## HOLE #3 SWING KEYS:

Do you have the clearest picture of your goals in mind?

In golf it is the flagstick and the hole that combine to give us the picture of our goal. The flag indicates the direction we should strive to send our shot toward, while the hole gives us the finality of the distance required to achieve success.

If there is no finality, make your goals clearer. It is not enough to have mere direction. Ensure that you have a purpose (direction or pin) and an ultimate destination (final success, or the hole) in mind.

# HOLE #4 PAR 4:

## GOLFING WITH MY WIFE

FOR MANY GOLFERS READING this, the title of this hole will suffice to tell the story and allow me to move on to the next hole. Most men will, unfortunately, read "Golfing with My Wife" and reflect on suppressed memories of the most painful day they can remember in their entire golfing careers. But there is a lesson to be learned from joining your spouse on the course, and it doesn't have to be negative.

Many years back, and quite early in my marriage, I talked my wife into joining me for a pleasant day on the links. The temperature in early May in Northern California was enough to coax her out of the house, and I was looking for any way I could to play more golf. So after I agreed to do the dishes that night, she decided to put up with four hours on the course. Little did she know that I was going to turn her into a golfer.

My wife stayed in the cart reading a book during my warm-up and also during the play of the first three holes. Conversation was minimal at best and sounded something like this:

"Did you see that shot, Honey?" I asked.

"Oh, it was magnificent, babe," she replied.

"You weren't even looking. I hit the damn thing in the water."

"Well, the splash was nice."

I refused to ruin the day getting mad at my wife's apathy toward my favorite pastime. So I teed up another ball and finished the third hole.

As I returned to the cart, I asked, "Would you like to hit a shot on the next hole?"

She undoubtedly felt trapped by the question, but she relented to hit a tee ball on the next hole.

The fourth hole at Cypress Lakes is a dog-leg right, par four, with a small lake on the inside of the corner and waste areas to the right. I handed her a slightly used ball, and she got mad.

"I want a new ball. You're hitting new golf balls. Don't give me your old worn-out golf balls to hit!"

"Sweetheart, there's water out there, and you're new to the game. I don't have a lot of new golf balls that I can let you lose for me."

"I'm not hitting this worn-out piece of junk. Give me a shiny one or I'll just sit in the cart."

"Fine, here is a new Titleist Tour Prestige. Don't lose it!"

She teed up the ball a little too high, but I wasn't going to say anything else to her for fear of losing a different kind of ball. She waggled excessively and made an unbelievable pass at the ball. My jaw dropped. The ball sailed high into the air directly toward the corner of the dog-leg. The ball cleared the mound on the corner and ended up in the fairway about 80 yards from the green. She had just hit a Callaway strong four-wood over 205 yards. It was simply astonishing.

"Was that good or something?" She finally broke the silence.

"Good? That was amazing!" I couldn't believe the shot she had just hit.

My wife got back in the cart and didn't hit another ball that day. In fact, in the last ten years she has only been to the driving range three times and maybe hit a total of fifty balls in that entire span of time. The shot she hit that day would have made a golfer out of almost anyone on the planet, but not her. She was not excited or overwhelmed by the quality of that shot. The golf bug didn't bite.

It took me a long time to learn a lesson from this golf experience, but I did. Golf was my dream. A career playing and teaching the game was what I wanted. Golf does not interest my wife, and that's okay. No matter how much I might wish for her to take up the game so we can have a grow-old-together activity, I'll survive if she doesn't. We can all learn something from this, even if it's painful.

## HOLE #4 SWING KEYS:

Are you like I was? Are you trying to make someone fit in with your plan or make them live your dream?

I think the answer to a quality life is for us to embrace our dreams as our own and allow others to enjoy *their* own paths. Sometimes we try to mold and shape those around us into a certain way or walk of life. This will only push those people further from us.

When we allow others the freedom to be outside of our goals looking in, we usually find that they will cheer us on more than if we had pushed them toward the same path we wanted to take. Nobody enjoys anything done begrudgingly.

# Hole #5 Par 3:

## HOLE IN NONE

MAKING A HOLE-IN-ONE IS fun. In fact, I recommend that everyone who reads this book get at least one of them during his or her golf career. Every day, golf courses across the planet add new members to their hole-in-one club. Even with new "aces" being recorded, you still don't have far to go to find a golf buddy who will hold your hole-in-one in contempt because he hasn't had his moment yet.

I have enjoyed making a hole-in-one five times thus far in my career, and I'll get around to sharing one more with you, but the one I want to talk about now still brings up some tough lesson memories.

The day was just like any other at Tanglewood Golf and Country Club, in Milton, Florida. Several members met just before one o'clock to pick teams in the daily "money game." I can still see all their cringing faces as the teams were divided up. I was in a pretty bad playing slump but was still a captain, so I had the honor of having Dave C. pick my team for me (inside joke for my buddy Jared. You're welcome to come on out to the game and see for yourself how the picks go down).

I headed to the first tee, with Ron, Harry, Frank, and Doug. On paper, we were actually pretty good. Harry was still hitting it well, and if Ron could find his putter, then we would be unstoppable. My big concern was two members of another team, Harry and Smitty; those two guys put more pars on paper than a statistician at a US Open. If they got going, we were in for a tough match.

The mood was low because I was just not scoring well. I was three over through four holes, when we made our way to the 145-yard par three fifth. As I waited my turn to hit, I selected a nine iron.

When I stepped to the ball, Ron reminded me, "You're playin' with my money too, so why don't you do something?"

Great pre-shot interruption, but I swung anyway. I couldn't take my eyes off the shot. It was perfect. A second later, Ron was jumping up and down on the tee box, counting his winnings.

I remember so clearly the moment when everyone's mood changed that day. We knew we were going to win. A hole-in-one was unstoppable. I high-fived the guys and had them all sign the ball (which is sitting here next to me as I write this chapter).

The remainder of the round was garbage for me. I had four more bogeys, two birdies, and an "other." An "other" is when you play so poorly on a hole that you just pick up and hope the other guys on the team can cover for you.

We finished up and then posted our team scores on the dry-erase board in the card room. As all the other teams came in and posted their scores, I began to realize something: golf, like life, is the sum of everything you do, not just the "aces."

We lost every bet that day, because our total scores for the day just weren't good enough. Yes, I enjoyed my ace and, thankfully, Santa Rosa, Florida, was a dry county at the time, so it wasn't too expensive to buy drinks for my team. But the lesson I learned that day was my only reward.

## HOLE #5 SWING KEYS:

Are you living from high point to high point? Are you neglecting the little things that keep you on par at work, home, or school each day?

As my team learned that day, you can be "aces up" one minute and pockets empty the next. I am not saying don't have your moments, but keep pace with life as you go so that the valleys of life don't swallow up your mountains of success.

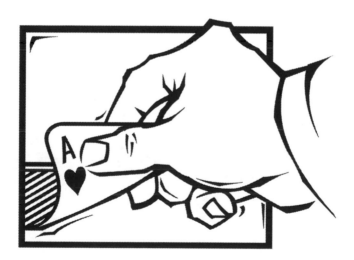

# Hole #6 Par 4:

## THE HOUSE ON THE CORNER

On one of the golf courses that helped shape my golf career there lives perhaps the nicest woman on earth. I have never heard her say a cross or disparaging word about anyone. Every time I have played golf with her, I have left the course feeling better about life; even if my round was not worth the paper my score was written on. This woman is not a bad golfer, either, but her medical-mission trips to help children in underdeveloped countries really put her time on the course in perspective. She enjoys the game, enjoys people, and is genuinely a good person. But, alas, this hole is not entitled "The Nicest Woman on Earth"; it is entitled "The House on the Corner."

Her house is two stories high and fits nicely in the golf course community, where it is nestled among the bunkers and the oaks on the inside corner of our dog-leg right par four. One would not find anything peculiar or magical about the place. It is a house of warmth. The porches, landscape, and white fencing blend together with an eye-pleasing country charm that invites you to ring the doorbell.

Ordinarily this house would not be awarded the attention I am granting it, except for one small fact: The house lies directly on the flight path of most drives hit on the hole. With visions of the grandiose, the daring golfer will attempt to cut the corner of the dog-leg. Pulling off the shot makes the hole an easy birdie or can even reward the brave with an eagle. All too often, and in the middle of the ball's flight, you'll hear the golfer yelling a request or two at his ball and praying that his ball doesn't hit Mrs. Nice Lady's house.

I hate to admit it, but I have found a few of my own golf balls in her yard as I've walked past the bunker hoping to find I'd cleared the corner. I've been very lucky, though, to have never hit the house or the beautiful new vehicle she got from her son. At least I've never *heard* my ball hit the house. The tree in the yard, that's a different story.

The last time I walked by, something about the house caught my attention. The siding on the tee-facing wall was pitted with holes and cracks. I didn't remember any weather reports about "hail-sized golf balls" near the course, so I knew I was looking at the remains of many golfers' broken tee-box dreams. The state of the exterior on this side of the house reminded me of another one of the life lessons that golf is ever willing to share. Very few of us contemplate the ill-effects our shortcuts "gone bad" might have on other people.

I thought back to how many times I had birdied the hole by just hitting the tee ball down the middle and not attempting the shortcut over the house on the corner. I could achieve my goals without bringing potential harm to the "Nicest Lady on Earth's" house. I know it's just one hole of golf, but what about in life? Who are your shortcuts affecting?

## HOLE #6 SWING KEYS:

I am not indicating that cutting a corner or taking the most direct route should be avoided at all cost. I am merely suggesting that personal gain achieved in the shortcuts we take is not the only facet to consider when making your decision to take the riskier path. In our climb-to-the-top society, far too many people are left on the sidelines, damaged by those who would catapult themselves to greatness regardless of the cost. Bring others with you on the journey; don't leave them in your wake. The celebration will be more fun when you enjoy it with more people.

# Hole #7 Par 5:

## TAKING THE PAT

I STARED EXCITEDLY AT the crystal vase sitting on my desk. It was a Sunday night in 2003. I had just won the Bitburger Land Club Championship. The trophy was magnificent. Though the scoring that year was higher than in preceding years, I had earned this trophy by grinding it out under the same conditions as everyone else. Mentally, I was beat. The wind had caused every player considerable troubles over the weekend, and I was actually relieved when the last putt fell and we could get off the course for a while.

Unfortunately, my triumph was short-lived. The next morning I was to take the Player's Ability Test, put on the by the Professional Golfers' Association of America. This playing test was the key to entering the Professional Golf Management Program, and I needed to pass so that I could start on the path to obtaining my Class A card. I put the trophy in the case and began to prepare mentally for the course at Heidelberg, where I would be tested.

The day of my PAT was conflicted from the beginning, and for the longest time it was the source of one of my greatest regrets, because it was my daughter's first day of kindergarten. If I was going to miss her first day of school, I had to make it count. I had to pass.

I didn't pass. I failed. I failed miserably. My putting was bush league at best. My driving would have been better if I'd turned around and hit left-handed. What I didn't know at the time was that I had placed so much pressure on passing that it was impossible for me to operate in what several golf authors have dubbed the *trusting mode*. I had just trusted my swing to victory in the days prior, but here I was abandoning myself, calling myself a bad father for not being there for my daughter, and mad at myself for not enjoying the win at Bitburgerland before moving on to the next step in my golf development.

As you can imagine, I could stop right here and go into the lessons learned just from the previous paragraph, but that would not allow us to capture the redeeming quality of golf. Stopping here would only get us as far as the failure: a young father making the wrong choice, an aspiring golf professional not recognizing the wear and tear from the tournament that would finally be on display during the playing test. Those lessons were tough to learn, but the toughest lessons have staying power.

Wait for it …

Redemption. This time it came in the form of a phone call and a simple question from my Dad.

"Did they take away your birthday?"

"What, Dad?"

"Joey, they didn't take away your birthday because you had a bad round. Your wife and daughter love you, and they're not after your birthday, either."

What my dad was saying—in his own special way, of course—was that the only failure in life is the failure in not trying. I would recover. I could and would be a great father every day, not just one. Most of all, he wanted me to know that the pressure I had heaped upon myself was wrong and that the PAT wasn't life and death. In fact, I have celebrated many more birthdays since that day, and the car ride home from the course at Heidelberg has long since been forgotten.

## HOLE #7 SWING KEYS:

Who are you giving your birthday to?

When we allow past failures to control our present happiness, we are literally giving away our birthdays. We are giving away our lives.

Don't give power to your failures. Learn from them and let them go. Recovery is a choice. All I want to do is be better today than I was yesterday. Golf taught me that, with a little help from my dad.

Keep your birthday—you were born with it!

# Hole #8 Par 3:

## Teaching Junior Golf

One of my great satisfactions as a teacher is watching a junior golfer hit the ball in the air for the first time. The reaction is pure joy. When a new golfer watches the ball sail through the air for the first time, the smile, the delight, and the "Did you see that?" are all so amazing to behold. It is in those moments that golf is growing. It is in that brief instant that I know golf will go on. When a junior "becomes" a golfer, I know golf is safe for the future.

The summer of 2009 provided the game with many new recruits. The junior program at Banyan Tree Golf Club was privileged to be a part of the development of over three hundred new golfers. Many of these still maintain an active lesson presence. Everywhere I went around the base that summer, I heard whispers of "that's the golf coach" or loud greetings of "hi, coach!"

I watched each day as the Okinawa summer heat, which often tops ninety degrees, with heat indices of over one hundred, didn't faze them. These children wanted to learn. The drills we taught them were mastered by some but tried and enjoyed by all. Their effort was clear. Several times I had to stop everyone from hitting while another young golfer, whose hands were dripping with sweat, slung his or her club downrange. It doesn't take long to sell out of junior golf gloves when you have over three hundred kids in your program.

In our camps, we wanted to keep the game a game. Personally, I think parents should take a hands-off approach with the game until a junior decides that he or she wants to be a better golfer. I provide the juniors with challenges and games that serve to keep them in the "fun zone." It is amazing to watch a young person learn something when they don't know they are learning.

As a result of these drills, I owed the class several push-ups each day. It was amazing to watch their determination to complete the different drills when my health was on the line. I had no clue that watching an overweight golf instructor do push-ups in the ninety-degree heat could motivate a junior golf class to knock fifty-yard shots within twenty feet of the pin. Last summer I lost count at 860 push-ups during week four of the nine weeks of golf camp. On a positive note, I did add fifteen yards to my own distance that summer, courtesy of this junior golf workout plan!

As a golf instructor, I pray that each junior program will be successful in ensuring the survival of the game. As a father, I consider each and every junior golfer an opportunity to teach and mentor skills to last a lifetime.

## HOLE #8 SWING KEYS:

The lesson here is simple. You know something—so pass it on. Mentoring is a great way to share the best of you with the future.

# HOLE #9 PAR 4:

## THE 280-YARD PUTTING STROKE

A RECENT TRIP TO Jacksonville, Florida, reminded me of a stupidly effective golf shot I made in 1995. I was a senior in high school in 1995 and did not quite have the talent to match my golfing aspirations. It was the week of the high school district golf tournament, and I was going to have a breakout week. I was so excited about the opportunity to right a rocky season with one good tournament. My plan was to play well, make the newspapers, land a scholarship, and head off to college. Oh, if only life were like the movies about life!

I was the co-captain of my high school golf team in 1995. We were not the worst team in the district, but the last tournament of the year was the first tournament of the year we would have team shirts. For a private school, we really didn't represent ourselves that well. I promise I'm over it now, some sixteen years later, but you have to admit a private school without matching team shirts is like a hunting club without a good dog.

The tournament did *not* go as planned. By the time I made it to eighteen, I had only one goal left that I could achieve. Coach had told the team, "If Joey breaks one hundred, I will buy dinner for the whole team." Yes, it is hard to admit to that statement being made about me, and to this day I am not sure whether coach was just trying to piss me off or if he just really wanted to buy dinner for us after the last tournament of the season. I was determined to *earn* my team some dinner. So I stood on the eighteenth tee and realized par meant dinner for the boys and me. I had hit my driver so poorly—actually, I had hit everything but my putter poorly that day—so I took out my (sorry, Mr. Solheim) Ping Anser 2 putter and hit my best tee shot of the day. When my playing companions stopped laughing, they realized that I had just out-driven them with my putter.

I don't remember his name, but the remark still stings: "You've been teeing off with the wrong club all day."

There it is: a lesson—a stupid shot and a lesson all at the same time. Well, at the same time if you don't count the lesson part of it coming till around fifteen years later. I learned something that day that only made sense when I later revisited the scene of the crime. (I am sure the good folks at Ping would consider it a crime, anyway.) The lesson is that sometimes we get attached to the wrong way of doing things. Sometimes we get "married" to our drivers, when a 280-yard putt is all that is needed. Oh, and yes—the pizza tasted good that night.

## HOLE #9 SWING KEYS

I have met a lot of business owners who ride their businesses into the ground because they get "married" to their way of doing things. I think the most successful people are able to adapt more quickly and don't let their feelings get hurt if their way isn't the best way. Sometimes the wrong tool for the job is the right tool—you just haven't defined the job correctly.

# Hole #10 Par 5:

## A NEW NINE

"All right boys, a new nine."

Other than "Fore!" and words not quite fit to print, "a new nine" could be the most-used phrase in golf. It seems the very design of our favorite game is all about redemption. We have a front nine, which most weekend golfers are so ready to forget, and a back nine, which for at least one shot, we are so ready to embrace. Golfers crave a chance to save the day. We would probably have far fewer golfers if it were called the front eighteen.

I have often stood on the tenth tee, with somewhere around thirty-nine to forty-one strokes for the front nine, trying to figure out how to save my score and my wallet. It seems that the farthest I have come in letting things go in golf is letting go of the front nine. Every golf psychologist in the world says you have to have a very short memory to play this game well. "Play one shot at a time. The most important shot is the one you're about to hit," they say.

Well, that's all well and good, and I'll keep working on it. For me, just like many others, the turnaround at the tenth tee is the place where my game seems to find itself. I don't know what it is about the tenth tee that gets my game fired up. Maybe it's that tasty beverage from the snack bar (because I would never sneak my own stuff out on the course), maybe it's the formality of changing from "out" to "in," or maybe golf is just that much like life …

The tenth-tee box of my life came July 14, 1998. I became a father. Fear, excitement, and amazing love were all running through me. I looked at my wife and held my brand-new daughter. I couldn't believe how lucky I was to be holding perfection. That little girl had me wrapped around her finger from moment one, and I just knew I had to put the mistakes of my front nine behind me. I had to be a better man, father, and husband. I had to play this back nine with everything I had. They deserved my best, and three-putting my way through life wasn't getting it done.

Just like the back nine of golf, things don't always match the plan we have on the tenth tee. The bogeys keep coming, the shots get farther right, and the scores head higher. In trying to play the back nine all at once, I failed miserably again. In failure I found the lesson. In failure I found success. Life is not a set of nine-hole matches. Life is every shot you take. Life is the good and the bad, the pre-shot routine and the post-shot elation or swear-word. Life, just like golf, is the sum of everything you do. But just like golf, life gives you more than one opportunity to turn it around. Every shot, every moment, is a new chance, a new opportunity to be great. I guess there is something to that sports psychology mantra, "The most important shot is the one you're about to hit."

## HOLE #10 SWING KEYS:

Are you trudging along waiting for the "tenth-tee box of life?" Are you going through the motions and just waiting for one big event to turn things around? If you learn nothing else from our time together, learn this: play every shot in golf as if it might be your last, and live every experience in life to the fullest.

A friend of mine named Doug signed my high-school yearbook thus: "Joey, live your life with no regrets." We can all say it's too late for that, or we can wake up each day and decide to live today with no regrets. Prisons are full of regrets, hearts are filled with regrets. Today is the day. You don't need a "new nine" to start over.

# HOLE #11 PAR 3:

## THE WORST SHOT EVER HIT

IN GERMANY ONE CAN find several golf courses with historical ties, and Rheinblick Golf Course in Wiesbaden is no different. A local once told me that the course served as training ground for Hitler's tank forces. You can also find light poles, should you hit your ball far enough into the woods, from the time when the course was a functioning ski resort. It is this attribute that gives the nickname heart-attack hill to the ninth (used to be eighteenth) hole. The legend of heart-attack hill grows every year, because the number of heart-failure-inducing walks up the steep grade seems to climb faster than the players making their way up the ominous fairway. I have never seen official records showing any heart attacks on heart-attack hill, but I have felt the calf-burning pain too many times myself not to believe some of the legend. But all of this past history of the course dimmed for an instant one Sunday morning in 2002, when the worst shot in the history of golf was recorded on the eleventh hole.

I was playing with the Dogfighters, a men's golf association, at Rheinblick Golf Course. I was struggling through my round and would not make a dime, Euro, or even a Deutsche Mark on this day, pending a major miracle. My group arrived at the eleventh hole, and I can only imagine the other players in the group were wishing to be paired with someone else. I can't really ever remember a round where I apologized for my play bringing down the other players in the group, but that day could have been a first.

I watched the other players in the group hit their tee shots, and none of the three men's shots found the green 175 yards away from us. After assessing their misfortune and the wind, I grabbed my Ping five iron and made a horrible golf swing. I pull-hooked the golf ball sixty-five yards left of the green. I watched in horror as the ball headed up toward the "winter" green.

33

The other members of my group watched in horror as the ball kicked off the bank next to the winter green and rolled down the cart path, down the hill, onto our green, and into the hole.

The guys went nuts. Some of the guys were hollering because they realized I'd be buying drinks for them. The other guys were swearing because, by the rules of our association, a hole-in-one trumps every other "skin"—so I had just taken the entire side pot for the day.

I know one thing. The worst shot ever hit in golf put money in my pocket and a story that will never be forgotten in a lot of players' memory banks.

## HOLE #11 SWING KEYS:

I have finally come to terms with the worst shot I ever hit. I know now that the mystique and peculiarities of golf were waiting for me on that tee box that day. I was to be taught a lesson. My eyes were to be opened that day to a facet of life that I still carry with me. It would be easy to say, "It's better to be lucky than good."

But I truly believe the lesson here is: You can prepare yourself to death. Sometimes you just have to get in the game, take your shot, and hope that it's good enough.

That day at Rheinblick, my shot was good enough to make history.

# Hole #12 Par 4:

## FAMILY GOLF TRIPS AND THE MOST IMPORTANT TROPHY

Every year, many golfers take group golf trips. I am sure, if you have played long enough, you are familiar with the fun, the food, and the backache-inducing, play-more-golf-in-a-week-than-most-people-play-all-year kinds of trips golfers take to places like Myrtle Beach or Vegas. (They say, "What happens in Vegas stays in Vegas." All I know is that the golf balls my dad takes to Vegas stay in Vegas).

My family started our yearly golf trip to get away from the business of life and to gather together for a week of catching up. We added the J. S. Lang Memorial Cup to our trip to honor my great-grandfather's memory. The cup is given to the lowest-total-score winner (net) based on three rounds of golf during the week. Aside from this, our family is no different than any other group of traveling golfers. We look for the best deals, try to play the best courses in the area, and hit more restaurant buffet lines than a Chris Farley lookalike convention. It is usually a great time to reconnect with family and friends around the favorite pastime of those attending.

It wasn't always a reconnect for me. In fact, one year I sort of disconnected with a family member during the trip. We were playing at a course near Myrtle Beach (Coastal Carolina University Course), and one of my uncles seemed to have a tendency that day to make all of his noise during my shots. My rabbit ears were standing tall, and I heard everything he did. Being overly competitive at what is supposed to be a fun golf outing is not a good thing. I brooded on this for the first two days of our trip.

On the evening of the second day, we were all gathered in the condo, and I made some stupid remark. My uncle told me that I didn't understand the meaning of this trip and I was disrespecting the memory of my great-grandfather with my selfish behavior. He said I was ruining the week for everyone and that I really needed to reflect on my attitude. I don't know anyone who takes criticism well in private, let alone in front of the rest of the family. Needless to say, I was in shock.

The remainder of the trip was uneventful. I didn't win the cup, and in fact, I have yet to win the cup. My only souvenir from this trip, besides a John Daly ball mark from Wicked Stick Golf Course, was sore pride. It took me quite some time to gather myself after this trip.

When I finally got over my initial soreness, I started to try to view things from my uncle's perspective. I had to admit that I had been wrong. I was being a jackass (in my own words, not his, although I didn't really give him an opportunity to use those words). So I had to humble myself and write a response to my uncle. I relayed to him my better understanding of our family trip. I told him I was a competitive golfer but that I knew that that week was supposed to be less about competition and more about connection. I told him that I knew everyone was not at the same place in their game and that was okay. I promised to work on my attitude and to always try to be mindful of the real reason we gather each year.

My uncle responded to my letter with an apology of his own. He said that he realized that I was a competitive golfer and the whole situation could have been handled better. My uncle displayed great character at that moment by accepting my apology and extending an olive branch of his own. I do plan on winning our family major this year, and I hope that my uncle will be there to see it happen. More importantly, I know now that by honoring my great-grandfather's memory, everyone wins every year.

## HOLE #12 SWING KEYS:

The lesson golf teaches here is to focus on what really matters. In golf, each shot is a distinctly different event, with its own set of objectives and variables. It doesn't matter how or why the ball got to where it is. It only matters where the ball needs to go from there. Far too often we get in our own way, too blinded by our own desires, efforts, and past experiences to realize that sometimes the agenda of the moment is not our own. We must learn to live each moment as a distinctly different event. When we learn to separate the important from the irrelevant, we will find more success in each moment of life than we ever thought possible.

# Hole #13 Par 5:

## GOLFING WITH JARED

In Northwest Florida lives one of the longest hitters of a golf ball on the planet. His name is Jared "this-one-guy-watched-me-hit-a-golf-ball-and-said-the-F-word-seven-times-before it landed" Floyd. I had the great honor of traveling to the RE/MAX World Long Drive Championship a few years back with Jared. This event showcases the longest hitters in golf. On display are some unusual and amazing attempts to violate a golf ball beyond the realm of human understanding. But I am not writing about the RE/MAX. I am writing about a casual round or two that I have played with Jared.

At Tanglewood Golf and Country Club, it was hard for me to go more than an afternoon or two without playing in the daily money game. Every day captains are chosen and the teams are divided up as fairly as possible. In all the days I have played in the game, I have only had Jared on my team a couple of times. This only happens when Boo Weekley or Bubba Watson are in town, so to make it fair I get Jared as my first pick. It is always fun to play with Jared, but one day I began to notice something I call the Jared Phenomenon.

On the afternoon I am reminded of, I began to notice myself swinging harder, trying to keep up with Jared. Can you believe that? How absurd. This guy hit it 396 at the World Long Drive Championship—and I am trying to keep pace with him! But it wasn't just me. I could see the other players in our foursome, Jeff M. and Dave C., also trying to swing harder and hit it farther, just to be like Jared.

There is only one problem with trying to play someone else's game. It's not yours! When you try to be someone else, you are telling yourself, "I don't trust me, so I need to swing like someone else." This totally invalidates all the time and energy you have spent refining your own personal move at the ball. Is your swing textbook? I don't know, but it's yours. Our bodies grow accustomed to the moves we program in. Furthermore, it is easier to derail a round of golf by attempting to play outside of your groove. Hence the phrase "my swing felt like a train wreck today."

It appears I may have made this book's "thirteenth-hole" play shorter than the third hole at Tanglewood for Jared. It is a 317-yard par four that I have seen Jared reach with a four iron. I can't even imagine what would be left of my back if I tried to make a swing like that. So I will leave Jared to his game, and I will stick to mine.

## HOLE #13 SWING KEYS:

The lesson here is a simple one: In life and in golf, be who you are. Your golf swing will thank you for it!

# HOLE #14 PAR 4:

## A PERFECT PLACE FOR A REFRIGERATOR

THE GREATEST OASIS ON the planet (for golfers) used to be found on the fourteenth hole at Tanglewood Golf Course in Milton, Florida. Much like Pavlov's experiments with dogs, I would find myself salivating on the fourteenth-tee box, knowing a trip to the *fridge* was coming. I know I am not alone in this anticipation. If you look at the divot placement in the fairway, it seems everyone hits it to the right to get a little closer to the fridge.

After you hit your tee shot, it would be time to make your way onto Mr. Nelly's porch. There a golfer could open the door to beverage nirvana. Mr. Nelly had more variety of drinks than the Circle K Gas station a block from the course. There were no prices on anything. Some people left money, some people didn't. I always left some cash, unless I was playing with Nelly, in which case I learned my money was no good at his place and I should stop leaving it.

The fridge always seemed to come at the perfect spot in my round. I would be both playing really well and starting to rush to the finish or I would be playing poorly, and a trip to the icebox would distract me enough to get it back together. Either way, Nelly's fridge had a path worn to its door by golfers of all types just looking for a momentary break from the grind of Tanglewood.

I recently returned to Tanglewood before heading to Ramstein Air Base in Germany. I had the chance to play with friends, but a trip to the fridge was not possible. All of the unofficial stops along the course had been removed. I heard they had been taken out, for one reason or another. Everything has its place in time and then it's gone. That fridge was definitely a welcome stop along the way. The funny thing about Nelly's fridge is how conditioned the golfers became. Most of the divots are *still* on the right side. You might say that is because most golfers slice. I say it is because most golfers at Tanglewood still want to head over to Nelly's for an Orange Slice.

## HOLE #14 SWING KEYS:

Change happens! Learn to embrace change. I think many people will agree that a co-worker's last job must have been better, because all you ever hear is, "We used to do it like this over at …"

The only thing I can say to that is how much I would still like to grab a cold beverage at Nelly's, but I can't. I can only tip my cap when I walk by and maybe recall some better moment. But I'll still have a few holes to play and a cold drink will be waiting at the clubhouse.

# Hole #15 Par 4:

## MY BEST TEACHER

THE WOODLAWN MEN'S AND ladies' golf associations partner on two events each year, with the spring and fall Jack and Jill tournaments. They are "social" golf outings, designed to help each group get to know the other and help grow the camaraderie of golf at Woodlawn. The format for the spring event was modified alternate shot. I don't know who picked this format, but my thanks are unending. Because of this format, I found the greatest teacher ever.

In the days leading up to the event, the men's coordinator told me that the female signups for the tournament exceeded the men's. He asked me if I would sign up to play so that they could balance the teams. How could I say no? As president of the men's golf association, I didn't have the option of saying no. I said yes and prayed for a little luck on the partner draw.

The polite woman manning the check-in table told me I had been paired with Ms. Ruth. When I met Ms. Ruth I thought my prayer had been denied. By the end of the day I would learn otherwise. I would come to know that this was a tournament only by name. The scores would all be ridiculously high, and everyone would smile through it.

Modified alternate shot means that both players hit a tee ball and the team selects the best one to play from there. If we chose my drive, then Ms. Ruth would hit the second shot from that spot, and I would hit the third. We would repeat this activity until the ball was holed or double bogey, whichever came first. Mostly it was double bogey that came first.

I hit the ball extremely well that day, and Ms. Ruth kept apologizing for not hitting the next shot as needed. I kept telling her that there was nothing she could do that day that would cause her to lose her birthday (I don't just write these lessons, I try to live them). She could not believe how patient I was with her. I told her that it was merely a fun event and we should embrace the format of the event we were in.

The real test came on number two, which was our eleventh hole of the day. The second hole at Woodlawn is a 274-yard par four that is sometimes reachable with hybrid. It just plays short. On this day, I hit my tee shot four feet short of the putting surface. That meant we had no more than ten feet to the hole. The second hole has four greenside bunkers. One of the bunkers was six or seven feet to our right and maybe even slightly behind where my tee shot lay. So, naturally, I hit our third shot from this bunker. That's right—my partner shanked our second shot into the trap. I had thought about asking her to putt the ball, but I didn't even consider the bunker to our right to be in play, so I didn't say anything.

Ms. Ruth immediately began apologizing and I stuck to my patient stance. I told her repeatedly that it was fine. We were going to be all right. No worries. I hit the ball from the bunker and we slapped it around on the putting green until we made a six. It was amazing—272 yards in one shot! Three yards took five more shots.

After the round, stories similar to ours on number two were regaled throughout dinner. Each couple seemed to have had a few moments like that one of ours. One wife even joked that divorce was not an option but murder was a possibility. I can't imagine how their day went.

When Ms. Ruth heard that joke, she turned to me and said, "If you're as patient with your wife as you were with my play today, you must be a gem to be married to."

I maintained a smile, but almost immediately I knew what prayer had been answered. It wasn't mine—it was my wife's. She must have been praying for me to learn something that day. Ms. Ruth's words were like a gut punch. I knew I wasn't that patient. I felt like a fake. I felt like a fraud.

That evening I went home and asked my wife to sit down with me for a chat. I told her about my day. I told her that I had met the greatest teacher in the world. That day had been my toughest lesson.

## HOLE #15 SWING KEYS:

WHAT IS THE LESSON here, you ask? The easy words are tolerance, compassion, and patience. The tough part is how we choose to apply these. There I was, so patient and understanding of Ms. Ruth's golf game, but when my wife comes home after a long day and isn't as friendly as I think she should be, I blow up. We fight, we yell, we retreat to our own corners to be angry the rest of the evening.

How can I be so patient with a stranger but not show my own family the same, or even greater, compassion?

Maybe we should treat everybody like a stranger we have to play golf with for a day. I've never met a stranger on the golf course that I didn't have at least one drink with after the round.

# Hole #16 Par 3:

## UNFINISHED BUSINESS

Number nine at Eglin Air Force Base's Falcon Golf Course is a 210-yard par three. The hole is pretty breathtaking for a military course. The tee boxes and the green are separated by a deep ravine, with a creek running through the bottom. If you're not on a greens mower trying to prepare the course for the day's play, you can get lost in the view here. Altogether, the facility has thirty-six holes (The Falcon and The Eagle), a driving range, several well-stocked ponds, a great pro shop, and some of the best eats in the area for a quick lunch.

In 2005, I was the contract golf professional at Eglin. In order to supplement my teaching income, Mr. Elkins hired me to work maintenance from 5:30 a.m. to 9:30 a.m. five days a week. Paul Wargo was the superintendent of the courses and he allowed me to change cups and cut greens.

One morning, I was cutting the Falcon's greens using the seven-to-one pattern. We used a clock face to set the mowing pattern. This made daily changes easy and gave the greens mower operators a clear pattern to follow. Changing the pattern is good for the greens, as the mowers tend to put a lot of pressure on the green in certain directions depending on the contour of the ground.

This pattern was no different than the others, except it was my least-favorite mowing pattern for hole number nine. This pattern put you on the front edge more than other patterns, and it is a long way down to the bottom of the ravine.

As I was cutting the green, I would make each turn being cognizant of the rear tires' turning radius. I made a few passes and all was fine—until I swung the mower just a little bit too wide. The back tire hit a patch of grass that was quite slick with morning dew, and it lost all traction. The mower began sliding backward down the hill. I was terrified. I tried to correct, but the mower was unresponsive and kept sliding. A few more feet down the hill, one of the tires caught and spun the mower sideways. This quick turn threw me off the mower onto my shoulder. I rolled to my back and looked up to see the mower flipping over toward me. I quickly tucked and rolled out of the path of the mower. Fortunately, the roll bar performed as it was designed to and stopped the mower from tumbling any further. The auto-disengage function shut down the mower. The only thing I could hear at that moment of that summer morning was the sound of my own heart beating out of control.

I grabbed the radio and called for Paul to come out to the ninth green. He came out and helped me gather myself. He asked me if I was okay, and after I convinced him I was no worse for the wear, he turned his attention to the upside-down John Deere mower. We got the mower upright and cleaned up a little spilled fuel. The mower was inspected for damage and was fine. It started right up, and the crew finished cutting the greens without me. There is truth to their motto "Nothing runs like a Deere."

Shortly after the incident, I wrote a letter to the men and women of John Deere thanking them for being safety-oriented. I can remember thinking it odd that a mower would have a roll bar, maybe even chuckling that I would hate to see the greens with enough undulation for a mower to require a roll bar. I am so very glad my mower had one and that it worked as designed. I told the employees of John Deere that their dedication and commitment to safety and performance had kept me alive and that I would go home to my family that night because of their hard work.

A couple of weeks later, I received an invitation to speak at the John Deere plant in Carey, North Carolina. I accepted the invitation but ultimately did not make it to the plant because of severe weather at the Pensacola Airport on the day I was supposed to travel. The trip was never rescheduled, but my appreciation to them is still strong. I just never got to thank them in person.

## HOLE #16 SWING KEYS:

What can we learn from this accident besides that it is prudent to wear brown pants when mowing greens? The answer is simple. I wrote this chapter to complete unfinished business. This hole is more about thanks to the folks at John Deere. I never got to meet them in person, so I always felt I had a bit of unfinished business to attend to. It is silly, but unfinished business will pile up in your internal inbox until the smallest of things keep you from functioning at your true potential.

*Learning to Live One Golf Swing at a Time* doesn't mean not planning for the future. It means learning to complete things. It means keeping your internal inbox empty so you will experience less stress and feel more joy in life.

# Hole #17 Par 3

## The Island and My Dad

Golfing with my dad is often a truly unique experience for people. Due to so many years of wrecking his body playing football, his swing is—let's just say unorthodox. I have given my dad many lessons with drills that have worked for countless students, but his body just doesn't move the usual way. Broken legs and hands, dislocated elbows and shoulders heal differently and make normal golf moves difficult for those who have experienced these injuries.

The thing that doesn't change, no matter who the golfer is, seems to be the universal language of frustration when you are learning to play the game. I used to joke that my dad was the only guy who could have three golf balls in the air at the same time. He always used to say, "Hit 'till you're happy." I'll admit that beating my dad was tough early on, because three balls off the tee and still making par is tough for anyone to beat. I never worried about the rules with my dad. I was just glad to have him out there.

Eventually, my dad committed to learning the game and its rules. He got so involved that he started volunteering at professional golf tournaments. He even started taking me to professional events, like the Players Championship in Ponte Vedra, near Jacksonville, Florida. After he saw that course, there was no turning back. He was, and still is, an addict of the sport. Will he ever shoot his age? I don't know and I don't care. I will say he gets a little closer every birthday. Golf with my dad has become fun over the last few years, and I will really miss his company on the course when he is gone. He has caddied for me on a couple of occasions, and whether I win or lose, we have an amazing time.

In 2007, we had the opportunity to play TPC Sawgrass together while working a project in the Jacksonville area. It is such a great course, but all day long you know what is coming. The island is waiting for you. No matter how you are playing that day, the island, with its mystique, is out there in the middle of that lake awaiting your best effort to tame it into submission. You approach the seventeenth-tee box from the sixteenth green, and your mind envisions all of the spectators that are there during the tournament watching the professionals play. Just like a kid, you imagine yourself walking up to the seventeenth needing birdie to give yourself a cushion going into the last hole of the Player's Championship. The buildup to that shot, even when there is no one there to watch it, is like no other shot in golf.

I had made birdie on the sixteenth, so I hit first on seventeen. I hit a nine iron, and my ball was safely on the green. I may have made a little remark or two, but my dad was unfazed by my trash talk. He grabbed his nine iron and hit a brand-new Pro-V1 (he said he would not be intimidated into using a lake ball here) to about eight feet. We were playing with a member of the course, who told us that was the best shot anyone in one of his groups had hit in a long time. My dad threw another ball down and told me to hit another as well. We both hit the green a second time. It was a pretty cool experience.

So my dad is two-for-two on the island green at TPC Sawgrass. In the years since, I have sat with him to watch the Players tournament on television, and I could see the joy cross his face when a pro hit it to where he did on the green—or, better yet, when a pro hit it into the water. I knew he wasn't cheering for them to splash down, but I think he enjoys having a perfect record for hitting the green there.

## HOLE #17 SWING KEYS:

I once heard that life isn't the "breaths you take but the moments that take your breath away." Throughout this book, I have tried to share lessons from my own golf experiences and relate them to life. This time I just want to say it's all right. Enjoy the moment. Take it all in and store it in the memory banks. When friends and family leave you, those memories will be all you have. Do your very best to have adequate moments to recall when the time comes. I've never heard of anyone on his or her deathbed saying "I wish I'd spent more time at work."

# Hole #18 Par 5:

## THE GREATEST COURSE IN THE WORLD

During my Air Force career, I was privileged enough to play the greatest golf course in the world. I know you're thinking Pebble Beach, Augusta, or St. Andrews, and rightfully so. But to me, the greatest course in the world lies on a small peninsula on the island of Cyprus. The Princess Mary's Hospital Golf Club is located on Royal Air Force Base, Akrotiri. It is here I learned one of the greatest lessons about the nature of golf clubs that anyone—not just a golfer—can learn.

The course is not that different from your average municipal course. There are tee boxes, greens, a club house, and a nineteenth hole. The most notable differences are: the tee boxes are concrete with rubber strip mats on top, the greens are "browns" (a mixture of oil and sand), and you have to carry your own "turf" with you to hit your ball from—because the course is built on top of a coral head that is exposed in many places, with very little grass available to hit from. In the summer, temperatures exceed one hundred degrees quite often, so a dip in the beautiful blue waters of the Mediterranean Sea is very inviting.

After that description of the course, you may never pony up the dough to get over and play TPMHGC—but you would be remiss. When I spent some time on the island, I stumbled upon the course, and in doing so I found the greatest collection of folks I would ever come to know. They welcomed me into their club as if I were a longtime member. They taught me how to get to know a golf course—how to read the intricacies of a place so unique that you had to accept the fact that a perfectly struck ball just might carom out of bounds. One of the members even gave me piece of Astro Turf so that I might be able to play the course without ruining my clubs.

I sat with them at the nineteenth hole, fascinated by old war stories and new golf stories. They told me the history of the base and of the club. They even helped me deal with the mosquitos of Cyprus (I called them two-hit wonders because you couldn't kill them with one hit). They were a refreshing bunch. It wasn't fortune or status that made you popular with them. They didn't even care if you hit the ball straight (because even straight balls get in trouble at TPMHGC). They only cared that you cared, that you respected the game, that you took delight in striking a little white ball, whether it be seventy times or over a hundred.

I even managed to play in a tournament with them during my time on the island. I finished second gross in my flight, and you would have thought I had won the Masters. The members were so delighted with my second-place finish. They smacked me on the back; they hooted and hollered. It was the best second-place finish I ever had.

## HOLE #18 SWING KEYS:

Hole eighteen brings us to a close on our first round together. Hole eighteen provides a look at the most important lesson of all in life. That is: people make the difference. People make a club, make a workplace, make a church, and make a school what it is. A scenic location does not a successful golf club make. It isn't enough to be fancy or beautiful or well maintained. You must have the people to have something real.

Don't forget the human element in your life. Get to know people. Enjoy their company. Make a difference in someone else's life, and a difference will be made in your own.

In short: don't play golf alone. Now, let's go grab a drink at the nineteenth hole.

# THE NINETEENTH HOLE:

## SETTLING UP

THE NINETEENTH HOLE IS the most common name for the bar golfers head to after the round. It's the place where bets get settled and stories get longer. It has a near-mythical status in golf. Ask a non-golfer to meet you at the nineteenth hole, and you will get a blank stare. You don't even have to ask a golfer to meet you; he or she is already there waiting on you to put your clubs in the trunk and grab a bar stool.

One day in 2009, there was to be no settling up. No money changed hands that day. I had played a round at Banyan Tree Golf Course with a good friend of mine named Brad. Brad is one of the good guys. He is a man of his word and will do for anyone before thinking of himself. He is just not someone who would play golf for a whole lot of money. If you got five dollars from Brad on the course, you were somebody. He's the only guy I know who can routinely pay off golf bets with under-the-couch-cushion change.

This day Brad would only teach me a lesson. I wouldn't even get any couch coins. I had beaten Brad out of five dollars through eighteen holes, and he said, "Let's go to the hundred-yard marker on eighteen and hit one shot for double or nothing. Closest to the pin wins." Having played well that day, I agreed.

We made our way to the marker and flipped a coin to see who would hit first. I won the toss, so I hit first, wanting to put some pressure on my buddy. I hit the ball, and it came to rest no more than two and a half feet from the hole. If Brad knew he was in trouble, he didn't show it.

Brad hit his shot dead on line with the pin. I watched in agony as the ball bounced once and then disappeared into the cup. I was in shock, and even though he acted as if he'd planned it, Brad was in shock, too. He had just scraped his way out of paying me with one of the most brilliantly timed shots in golf.

## THE NINETEENTH HOLE SWING KEYS:

Brad is a good friend, and the story is worth more than the ten bucks that double or nothing could have won me. If I had settled with Brad for five dollars, I would have missed out on the best shot of his career. But I would have had five dollars from Brad.

So, decide what is important to you and go for it. Don't settle for less, but be prepared for anything in this journey. You might lose five bucks—or you might be witness to some pretty cool moments along the way.

# Afterword

So there you have it. I don't know whether *Golf Digest* will rate this course with four stars, but your life should definitely be on their "Places to Play" list.

It is my hope that by using the lessons in this book you will learn not just to enjoy the game of golf more but to embrace the life within you. It is yours, and it's up to you to get the most out of it that you can.

Maybe one day the starter will pair us together on the first tee somewhere. If not, just know that I am doing my best to play this game one shot at a time.

Are you?

# About the Author

Joey started teaching golf in 1999 at Travis Air Force Base's Cypress Lakes Golf Course. Since then, he has been a contract golf instructor at Eglin Air Force Base and Kadena Air Base, Japan. He is currently out there somewhere preparing for another go around on a mini-tour and annual US Open qualifying. Joey lives with his wife and daughter in Northwest Florida.

# COMING SOON

*Learning to Live One Golf Swing at a Time: Walking with Champions*

Follow Joey as he interviews past tour champions about their own "Learning to Live" moments. Players will share stories of triumph, tragedy, love, and loss from life's majors.

*Learning to Live One Golf Swing at a Time: Moments with the Fans*

Digging deep into the fan mail, Joey takes a look at the casual golfer's love/hate relationship with the game of golf.